THE
WELLNESS
BOOK

BY JOHN RANDOLPH PRICE

Books
*The Abundance Book
Angel Energy
The Angels Within Us
*Empowerment
Living a Life of Joy
*Practical Spirituality
*A Spiritual Philosophy for the New World
*The Success Book
*The Superbeings
*The Wellness Book
*With Wings As Eagles
*The Workbook for Self-Mastery

Selected Audiocassettes
*Flight of the Eagle
*The 40-Day Prosperity Plan
*Global Mind Link/World Healing Meditation
*A Journey into the Fourth Dimension
*The Manifestation Process
*Prayer, Principles & Power

Check your bookstore for the books and audios above.
Items with asterisks can be ordered through Hay House at
800-654-4126 • FAX: 800-650-5115

Please visit the Hay House Website at:
www.hayhouse.com

The
Wellness
Book

JOHN RANDOLPH PRICE

Hay House, Inc.
Carlsbad, CA

Copyright © 1998 by John Randolph Price

Published and distributed in the United States by: Hay House, Inc.
P.O. Box 5100, Carlsbad, CA 92018-5100
(800) 654-5126 • (800) 650-5115 (fax)

Edited by: Jill Kramer   *Designed by:* Jenny Richards

Library of Congress Cataloging-in-Publication Data

Price, John Randolph.
    The Wellness Book / John Randolph Price.
            p.   cm.
    Includes bibliographical references.
    ISBN 1-56170-500-4
    1. New Thought.   2. Spiritual healing.
    3. Health—Miscellanea.
    I. Title.
    BF645.P87   1998
    299' .93—dc21   97-47697
                                                            CIP

                    ISBN 1-56170-500-4

            01 00 99 98   4 3 2 1
            First Printing, May 1998

                Printed in Canada

Dedicated to the healing and harmonizing of minds and emotions, thus revealing physical wholeness—and to the truth that nothing is impossible

❧❧ CONTENTS

❦ Introduction

*T*he *Wellness Book* is the third in a series of small, easy-to-carry volumes—a collection of my writings on health and healing similar in style to *The Abundance Book* and *The Success Book.*

Throughout the Ancient Wisdom texts, we read that ideal health is the natural way of life— that our physical bodies were created according to the perfect pattern and are maintained in wholeness from birth until it is time to make our transition to a higher plane of life. However, someone born with an affliction, or one who has continued to suffer from some form of chronic disease, may find that hard to believe.

The fact of the matter is that when we took on form in the third-dimensional experience, our bodies were perfect, and we could come and go from one plane to another simply through the process of dematerialization-materialization. But in time we began to identify with our physical bodies, slowly entered the sleep state, and lost our conscious awareness of the Truth—that we are pure spiritual beings, forever one with the Master Vibration of Perfection, our Essential Self.

When death was created by the collective human mind as a way of dropping the physical body, we took our consciousness with us—and when we returned to this dimension through the process of reincarnation, we brought back the basic shape and tone of consciousness of our previous life experiences. If we had not realized our wholeness and perfection before, we came back to try again—perhaps bringing with us certain vulnerabilities to overcome. Could we not find that perfect pattern while on a higher plane? No, because our body was one of sculptured light rather than a fleshly form. So we returned to this so-called material existence to awaken more fully to our Divine Consciousness—not only to realize physical perfection but also to fully understand the beauty and fulfillment of ideal relationships, ideal abundance, ideal success, and every other aspect of living the perfect life. And this is all accomplished through a deeper awareness, understanding, and knowledge of who and what we are. It is an awakening to the Truth of Being, which must be done on the plane where we fell asleep.

Regarding physical healing and maintaining the body in wholeness, I not only believe that all things are possible, but that we *already* live in a state of physical perfection. The body has no power to create sickness, and there is nothing in the outer world that can harm it; therefore, in truth, there is nothing to heal in the physical system. It is our thoughts and emotions in the form of false beliefs that have superimposed a false pattern, an illusion that we judge to be discomfort, sickness, and disease. Accordingly, we focus on untying the knots of those beliefs and transforming reactive emotions into positive feelings of love, joy, and peace. In essence, when the points of friction in our energy field are healed, the body responds in like manner—and we experience the revelation that the body vehicle is well and strong. It was all the time, but we were seeing a false body through emotional eyes and a distorted personal sense.

We will look at different techniques, methods, and processes to change our attitudes about life on the material plane, to lift consciousness above the appearance of maladies and illness, with the grand objective of realizing that there is only one presence and power in this universe—the *I* of our

Divine Identity. As we do that, the Ideal Life will be revealed to us—a life without karmic debts, discord, conflict, scarcity, failure, and certainly without afflictions, ailments, and infirmities.

It is time to become whole and strong again—as we were created to be—so that we may fulfill our purpose for being.

Let's begin now.

~ 1
The Way of Health

Patrick M., an M.D. specializing in family practice, says that a growing number of doctors agree that there is a healing power within us and that it is possible for this power to maintain the body in perfect condition. He said, "I, personally, believe that this spiritual life-stream will keep the body in a state of perfection when man realizes the unreality of disease."

The unreality of disease. A strong statement for a medical doctor who daily sees an endless parade of patients with some form of illness or suffering. But Patrick M. is no ordinary doctor. He is a Superbeing who also happens to have found his true place in the medical profession. Dr. M. believes that all body malfunctions are the result of negative patterns lodged in the subconscious mind. Don't talk to him about viruses or bacteria or heredity. Do so and he will counter with a discussion of fear patterns, emotional instability, and mental conflicts.

"I treat the cause as much as I do the effect," he said. "Without oversimplifying it, you could say that high blood pressure, for example, may be an indication of a subjective pattern laced with feelings of irritation, resentment, and criticism. The common denominators of most illnesses, in my opinion, are confusion, fear, resentment, futility, hostility, and irritation. As we replace these 'bugs' with healing thoughts, they are cast out, and the body resumes its natural harmonious functioning. Nature's built-in life support system, if not tampered with, will maintain the body in an ideal state."

Dr. M. is not alone in his thinking. Behavioral medicine has become a major field of study by an increasing number of physicians throughout the country. Medical researchers at such institutions as Johns Hopkins University School of Medicine, the University of Southern California, and Yale University are agreeing that *emotions* are the primary factor in illness. And in tracking a disease from its manifest state back through the body to the mental distress that set off the physical imbalance, these researchers are finding deep-seated patterns of anxiety, grief, anger, depression, and fear. In thousands of case histories, the evidence is clear: The body *does* reflect the state of an individual's emotions.

Holistic Healing

There is a definite trend in the medical profession to shift the focus from the repair of the physical mechanism to an improvement of the functioning of the whole being. This is the "holistic" approach to medicine, where the doctor considers the total interrelationship of mind, body, and spirit in creating a state of well-being in the individual. Part of the inspiration for this movement is the growing understanding that there is a healing principle within us that is the cause of our physical expression.

But we need to go further than this and realize that the Creative Mind that is individualized *as* us has no conception whatsoever of disease. This Mind is the Will of God in individual expression, and it sees and knows only perfection. Within its consciousness is the idea of the perfect body, and this Ideal Pattern is constantly seeking to renew the body after Itself. Science knows that every cell in the body is periodically renewed, so it is only logical to state that it is *consciousness* that alters the cells according to our thoughts and emotions.

"The body reflects the mind," says Dr. M. "When the mind is in tune with its Christ nature, it becomes harmonious, and this state of consciousness will maintain order in the bodily function. Disorder in the mind will disturb the equilibrium of the body."

So, again, mind is the answer! If you can see your body as your True Self sees it, your body will respond accordingly. If you can understand that your life is God's Life and that God's Life is perfect, then you can realize that the life form you are cannot embrace sickness or decay.

Preventive Medicine

To enjoy perfect health, you must choose and accept it. You must tune in to the Superconsciousness within you and let its healing power be released into every cell and organ of your body. Be conscious of the Life Force flowing through you. Feel its soothing, healing currents of divine love, and know that every function of your physical being is whole and complete. Embody the idea of perfect health in your consciousness, and you will be restored, renewed, and revitalized after the Perfect Pattern within.

Dr. M. makes an interesting observation:

> I have seen miraculous healings. . . terminal cancer disappearing without a trace and other instantaneous "cures" by what must be considered spiritual means. Many of these people were able to turn within, tune in, and release the healing power by effecting a change in consciousness. What puzzles me is this. If they were already advanced in consciousness to the point where the Divine Law of Adjustment could be called into play on such short notice, why did they let themselves become vulnerable to the disease in the first place? We should not wait until the body breaks down to practice spiritual health. We must let the Christ live through us each day of our lives. This is true preventive medicine.

Accept the Truth that you are perfect, and build the mental equivalent that nothing can touch your body except the direct action of God, and God is Love. Understand that God does not *give* you health...God *is* your health. Since you are one with Wholeness and Perfection, that must be the true state of your being.

Lift up your vision. See yourself as God sees you—radiantly healthy and filled with joy and peace. See yourself doing everything you want to do, energetically, enthusiastically, and easily. See yourself smiling, laughing, and expressing a new zest for living. Visualize your body as a dynamic vehicle for every physical expression that you enjoy doing, and see yourself demonstrating a wonderful sense of well-being. And most of all, keep your mind free of all thoughts of confusion, fear, resentment, futility, and irritation. Fill your consciousness with love, joy, peace, and gratitude.

Remember that 24 of Jesus' 33 miracles were related to the healing of the body. Also recall that he said, "He who believes in me will also do the works that I do; and greater works than these will he do." He is telling you that you can realize the healing principle if you put your trust in your indwelling Christ. He is saying that you, too, can heal if you believe in the Power of the Christ Mind within you. You can heal yourself—you can heal others—you can be a healing influence to all those within the range of your consciousness.

But remember the condition: "He who believes in me…" You must believe Wholeheartedly if you are to reveal the healing Truth. To do this you must replace error concepts of disease and convictions of imperfection with ideas based on the Reality of you—whole, perfect, and complete. To be healed and to enjoy radiant health on a continuous basis, you must introduce new affirmative thoughts into your consciousness…you must "change your mind" about your body.

Meditate daily on this Perfect You, and speak your word of healing with authority as Jesus did— regardless of what the condition appears to be.

Live the Truth of Health

After your meditation, go about your business with an uplifted consciousness of health and well-being. And remember, you have to *live* the truth of health. You cannot reprogram your consciousness on the mental level and expect it to remain open as a channel for the healing power if you do not continue your health work in the manifest world. This means that you cannot maintain a consciousness of health unless there is continuity between what you think and how you act. If you affirm a perfect body and then fail to exercise, diet properly, or eat the right foods, you are not practicing health.

Understand that exercise and diet will not necessarily promote good health. Rather, they may help you in the development of a *health consciousness*. And that's the key. You take whatever action in the outer world will give you a greater sense of well-being, greater confidence in the natural functioning of your body, and a more positive attitude toward the physical you. Remember that your body is an outpicturing of your deeper mind. It is a mirror image of what you sincerely believe about yourself, and your subconscious mind is constantly monitoring your beliefs. So if you affirm one thing and act in a different manner, the actions will speak louder than words and you will cancel out your good. In effect, you will be telling your subconscious to disregard the previous instructions and to continue believing in a less-than-perfect body.

For example, you affirm and visualize a body filled with great energy and vitality, but then you position yourself primarily on your posterior most of the day at home or in the office, overindulge in food and drink, get too little (or too much) sleep, and then complain because you are tired and not feeling very well. You've simply got to tie it all together—thought and action—if you want the creative concept of health to work.

The same holds true in reverse. You can jog five miles a day, eat only natural foods, take the limit of vitamins and minerals—and spend your days agitated, resentful, fearful, and wondering why you are not enjoying good health. Science has now traced 80 percent of all ailments to the way we think, and it will not be long before that figure is 100 percent. Five miles of jogging may not cancel out five minutes of hostility. And all the vitamins on the shelf simply will not overcome the physical damage caused by daily doses of resentment and unforgiveness.

You have got to get your *whole* act together in order to enjoy the radiant health that is your divine birthright. And never for a minute doubt that you can be healed of any disease. The Power within can cure a cancer as easily as a cold, but in order to readjust your bodily functions, it must flow through your consciousness. If the Power flows through a mental household littered with fear of living, or a fascination with illness, or a condemning heart, then it must duplicate or maintain that state of mind in your body. Your body reflects your mind. It is the physical image of your mental atmosphere. Now you can understand why some mental housecleaning will be necessary if your body is not everything you want it to be.

Should you visit a doctor if you are ill? Of course, if that is where you are in consciousness. And if you are not *sure* of your realization of the healing principle, combine medical assistance with spiritual healing treatments. Above all, do not try to demonstrate beyond the level of your consciousness. God may have to work through the physician and through you while you are working to correct the alignment of your soul. But once you have completed your mental cleansing and have realized the truth of health, you may never see a doctor again—except on the golf course.

How the Body Reflects the Mind

Subconscious patterns of:	May manifest as:
ANGER/HOSTILITY	Appendicitis, arthritis, boils, constipation, heart problems, high blood pressure, indigestion, inflammation
CONFUSION-FRUSTRATION	Colds, flu, headache
FEAR	Accidents, asthma, flu, headache, heart problems, indigestion

GRIEF/DEPRESSION	Cancer, colds, gallstones
GUILT, SELF-CONDEMNATION	Back trouble, cancer, hay fever
LACK/LIMITATION	Anemia, asthma, kidney trouble
OLD AGE CONCERN	Hardening of arteries, kidney trouble
RESENTMENT/ UNFORGIVENESS	Arthritis, cancer, heart problems
TENSION/STRESS	Colds, constipation, headache, high blood pressure

A Word about Age

The true Superbeings throughout the world are literally reversing the aging process. They have realized that the indwelling Reality cannot grow old, cannot age, cannot die—that the True Self of each individual lives in a perpetual state of eternal youthfulness. Since this is true, there must be an idea corresponding to this divine nature in the mind of each Superconsciousness. The advanced souls have recognized this idea and have appropriated it into their consciousness. The Law then works through this divine Pattern to slow down, stop, and reverse the aging process and reflect a younger and more vibrant appearance.

Never forget that what the mind can conceive and believe, the mind can achieve.

2

THE DIVINE VIBRATION OF WHOLENESS

All of creation—the infinite universes and all that is visible and invisible—is energy in motion. It is the Thinkingness and Knowingness of God-Mind—Divine Ideas in a state of continuous manifestation. The Spirit of God is pure Cosmic Energy, and this spiritual substance is individualized as each man, each woman. Therefore, each one of us is an energy field pulsating to a divine vibration. This is our Life Force—the pure Energy of God—and as this Energy lowers its rate of vibration, physical form takes place, manifesting as cells, tissue, and organs according to the Perfect Body Idea (the Word). And the Word is made flesh.

Ideas such as sickness, disease, and old age do not exist in the Mind of God. Therefore, as the pure

Energy of God-Mind expresses as the Life Principle and forms the body according to the Perfect Pattern, the visible manifestation must also be perfect. Since we were created out of perfection, we must be perfect. But how do we explain the appearance of disease and sickness? Go back to the principle that in the Mind of God, thoughts are creative, and since we are individualizations of God, our thoughts are also creative. We have the freedom to create conditions and experiences in our lives according to the thoughts we think and accept as true. Thus, we create our own diseases by objectifying fear, hate, worry, or other mental-emotional disturbances. But we can also be restored to our normal state of perfection through the right use of our minds.

Any idea that is registered as a conviction in our deeper mind results in a change in our world, beginning with the body. When we begin to consider that the healing principle within is the Cause of our physical well-being, the negative energy within our individual force field begins to change. In other words, physical perfection is the natural state of our being, and as this Truth is accepted in our thinking and feeling natures, our bodies will change accordingly. So a "healing" is simply a return to our natural state.

Based on my research into the subject of health and healing, I believe that an individual can return to his/her natural state of perfection by working with the four "bodies" that comprise individual being: the spiritual, emotional, mental, and physical bodies. In the spiritual realm we dedicate ourselves to realizing our True Nature by working from the vantage point that we are spiritual beings—to awaken to the truth of our Divine Identity. This is the purpose of meditation, where we dwell upon our inner Reality, knowing that whatever we contemplate is drawn into our consciousness. This focus on the Christ within will also begin to awaken the subconscious to "remember" the true Image of Self—the Divine Perfection we are. So meditation is the foundation for both a restoration and a preventive "medicine" program. Through meditation, you will be raising the vibration of your energy field to the divine frequency, thus opening the way for the healing currents to move through every atom of your being.

In working with the emotional body, do whatever is necessary to immediately rid yourself of all negative feelings such as unforgiveness, resentment, criticism, fear, and jealousy. Even the

American Medical Association is talking about the cause-and-effect relationship between emotions and wellness. In the January 14, 1983 issue of *The Journal of the American Medical Association*, it was reported that "…investigators found that gum-disease patients had experienced more negative, unsettling life events in the previous year than other people…they also demonstrated higher levels of anxiety, depression, and emotional disturbances."

We have found that the use of spiritual treatments can reverse deep-seated emotional patterns and clear a path for the Inner Power to act. For example, if there is unforgiveness in your heart toward anyone (a parent thought for arthritis, cancer, and heart problems), sit quietly and state firmly and lovingly: "I forgive you totally and completely. I hold no unforgiveness in my heart toward anyone, and if there is anything in my consciousness that even resembles unforgiveness, I cast it upon the indwelling Christ to be dissolved right now. I forgive everyone and I am free!"

Work with such statements, adapting and changing the words for any negative emotion, until you feel a sense of release and there is no longer a negative attachment to the person or experience.

When we come down to managing our thought

processes, we are actually working with the mental body. As Louise L. Hay says in her book *Heal Your Body*:

> Stop for a moment and catch your thought. What are you thinking right now? If thoughts shape your life and experiences, would you want this thought to become true for you? If it is a thought of worry or anger or hurt or revenge, how do you think this thought will come back to you? If we want a joyous life, we must think joyous thoughts. If we want a prosperous life, we must think prosperous thoughts. If we want a loving life, we must think loving thoughts. Whatever we send out mentally or verbally will come back to us in life form. Listen to the words you say. If you hear yourself saying something three times, write it down. It has become a pattern for you. At the end of a week, look at the list you have made, and you will see how your words fit your experience. Be willing to change your words and thoughts, and watch your life change. It's your power and your choice. No one thinks in your mind but you."[1]

Remember that the use of creative imagination and visualization techniques also relates to your mental body and greatly influences the physical system. See yourself well! Visualize your whole-ness, the natural state of your being. Cancer patients, for example, are benefiting from what is called "positive-image therapy." It combines relax-ation techniques with teaching the patient to imag-ine the body's natural cancer-fighting forces—the white blood cells, for instance—and to visualize that the cancer is vulnerable to the treatment. In a study at the Washington School of Psychiatry, six patients led by Dr. Robert Kvarnes had blood sam-ples analyzed before and after the training. The result was that the number of white cells and the amount of a chemical called thymosin in their blood increased. Both changes indicated that the patients' immune systems were stronger.

Spiritual Activity

Let's base our spiritual work on bringing the spiritual, emotional, mental, and physical bodies into perfect alignment.

Earlier I discussed the effects of meditation as a "foundation for both a restoration and preventive 'medicine' program." The form of meditation I am recommending here in order to realize the true nature of Wholeness is called a "meditative treatment." If you are experiencing a health problem, it means that there is a false belief in your consciousness that is outpicturing itself as a malady in your body. There is a misconception and a misunderstanding in your mind regarding the natural state of your being. To meet this challenge, you must replace the error with Truth in consciousness, and this can be done most effectively through this type of meditation.

This is the statement we will work with in the meditative treatment:

> *The Spirit of God is the Life Force within me, and every cell of my body is filled with the intelligence, love, and radiant energy of God-Mind.*
>
> *God's will for me is perfect health, and God sees me as perfect; therefore, wellness is the natural state of my being.*
>
> *Ideas such as sickness, disease, and old age cannot exist in the Mind of God. That Mind is my mind, so I now see myself as God sees me...strong, vital, perfect.*
>
> *I am now lifted up into the*

Consciousness of Wholeness. I accept my healing. I am healed now! And it is so.

Now become very still and relaxed, then slowly and with feeling, read the statement again, meditating on each word, contemplating each sentence until the true meaning registers in your consciousness. Remember that words are only symbols; it is the idea behind the word that has power. So meditate on the idea until there is an inner understanding and realization. I will lead you through the first meditation, but in subsequent treatments, let your own thoughts replace my words.

Meditation

The Spirit of God…(Contemplate the idea—the meaning behind the words—of the Spirit of God until you feel something within. Speak the words silently, and watch the other thoughts that flow in to expand your thinking.)

…is the Life Force within me…(Dwell on the meaning and the activity of the Life Force of God operating in and through your body. Feel the dynamics of this incredible power. Sense the

renewing, restoring action of Spirit as it eliminates everything unlike itself in your body.)

…and every cell of my body is filled with the intelligence, love, and radiant energy of God-Mind. (See each cell pulsating with Light and Life—filled with God-Intelligence, God-Love, and God-Energy. Each cell is now thinking the thoughts of God, expressing the Love of God, and vibrating in harmony with the peace of God. Contemplate this.)

God's will for me is perfect health… (Think of God's will as the cosmic urge to express perfection, which is being done in your body at this moment.)

…and God sees me as perfect… (This is the Vision of God projecting the Reality of Perfection throughout every cell, organ, and tissue of your body. Ponder this.)

…therefore, wellness is the natural state of my being. (What God sees is the Reality behind the illusion. This Divine Vision, this Holy Seeingness, is permeating your entire being. Feel this.)

Ideas such as sickness, disease, and old age cannot exist in the Mind of God. (If such ideas do not exist, they cannot be manifest; therefore, it is your ideas that have been expressed as a negative physical condition. You are now aware of this, and you know that you have the divine authority to replace those error thoughts with Truth ideas, and you now make the definite decision to do so.)

That Mind is my mind...(There is but one Mind—God-Mind. That Mind is in expression as your mind. Your mind, being a part of God-Mind, has the Holy Power of Spirit. And you are now using that Power in cooperating with God. Contemplate God's Mind expressing as your mind, and your mind expressing God's Ideas of Perfection.)

...so I now see as God sees me...strong, vital, perfect. (Lift up your vision and see as God sees. See Wholeness. See Wellness. See Divine Order. See Perfection. See God *as* your body.)

I am now lifted up into the Consciousness of Wholeness. (Feel the pure vibration of Love, Life, and Light as you rise into the very Presence of Spirit. Meditate on the spiritual energy that now surrounds you, engulfs you, and flows in and through you. Let go and give yourself to the magnificent healing currents.)

I accept my healing. I am healed now! And it is so. (When you accept your healing, you have taken the final step. Where there was darkness, there is now Light. Where there was error, there is now Truth. Where there was imperfection, there is now Perfection. You are healed! Acknowledge now that it is so.)

Remain in the consciousness of Spirit for a few more minutes, in communion with your God-Self. In this spiritual vibration, you will be highly successful in healing with your emotional body. Forgiving others will be easy, and old hurts, resentments, and other negative feelings can quickly be cast upon the Christ within to be dissolved. For this particular activity, make a list of everyone who could possibly need your forgiveness, then speak their name aloud and say: "I forgive you. I choose to do this now, and I hold nothing back. I forgive you totally and completely."

Next, take an imaginary box and in your mind, fill it with every hurt, resentment, condemnation, depressed feeling, anger thought, and any other negative patterns you find in consciousness. Take the box and see yourself lovingly placing it upon the Holy Fire of Spirit within where it is totally consumed.

To properly manage your thought process, refer back to the words from Louise Hay's book *Heal Your Body*, and begin to listen to the words you say throughout the day. What habit patterns are you forming? Start exercising control over the thoughts you think and the words you speak. Practice thinking joyful, loving, prosperous, and harmonious thoughts. Train yourself to think and speak only according to the Christ standard, and use your power of creative imagination to see yourself as whole, well, and perfect.

In working with the physical body, ask yourself: "What do I intuitively feel I must do in the manifest world to maintain my body in top physical condition?" Whatever the answer, be sure to follow your inner guidance in establishing a health program that is right for your individual consciousness.

Work daily to keep your four bodies in holy agreement, and sickness will be a thing of the past for you.

※ 3

HEALING THE RESISTANCE
IN CONSCIOUSNESS

To experience pain and sickness means that we have increased the amount of resistance in our electrical circuitry—and the higher the resistance, the less the flow of the healing currents.

The entire Universal Energy Field is electric, and everything that is manifest—including our physical bodies—is electrical. Science knows this, but what it doesn't tell us is that each individual energy field is composed of nothing but flowing electricity. And the electricity follows the Divine Circuits (Spiritual Patterns) to manifest forms and conditions matching the absolute quality of the Source. The electrical power flowing through us never thinks of anything but giving to the fullest measure of its capability, which is infinite. It knows nothing about those things in consciousness that resemble switches, fuses, or rheostats. The power is only conscious of being all that it is.

If any individual was sufficiently transparent in consciousness with no limitations imposed, and was completely clear of personal ego, the physical body would be so perfect that it would appear ethereal, and consciousness would appear so ecstatic that life would be nothing less than a rapturous adventure in all that is good, true, and beautiful.

The healing currents flowing from on High enter our auric field to produce Light, Heat, and Power. Light is *Illumination*, the central Spiritual Sun focused as the brilliance of knowledge, wisdom, and understanding. Heat is *Love*, the Cause behind all manifestation, the Cosmic Fire that creates new form and vivifies all things. Power is *Will and Purpose*, the authority to work in and with all energies to keep the circuits open and the magnetic force intact. With Illumination, Love, and Will, there is nothing we cannot do, be, or have—yet we continually live with gaps in the circuit, which stop the flow of the healing currents.

Looking at electricity in the mundane sense, the flow of electric current depends on its pressure, rate, and the resistance on the conductor to the flow. In the spiritual dimension, the divine electrical thrust (pressure) is absolute, unconditional, and unlimited. Its velocity (rate) is total and maximum—so infinitely faster than the scientific calculation of the speed of light that its creative energy is perpetually working in the *now*. Therefore, the pressure and rate are forever in a state of perfect, permanent, and unfailing givingness —the expression and manifestation of the ideal body. That leaves only one factor as the culprit—the resistance of the conductor—that is, the resistance in consciousness.

There are many reasons why we have switched off the healing current, caused breaks in the circuit with fuses, and dimmed the light with our self-created rheostats. One is through ignorance of our Truth of Being. We assumed that we were less than Divine—that we were condemned, victimized humans—and we consented to play that role on the stage of life. But thousands of years ago this lie was exposed, and on some level of consciousness within each individual, the Truth is known. Of course, it may be so deeply buried that only the animal nature is expressed, but even in this tomb of darkness, the spark of salvation is working, and someday those sealed vaults will open, and awakened ones will emerge.

There are also millions of people on the planet now who have at least an intellectual understanding of spiritual reality, and while they may continue to function as people with amnesia, they believe in the Truth, and they are working daily to awaken to their former state of Consciousness. And there are still others who have moved up the evolutionary ladder to the point of *realization*, where the Truth is known, and they are living as full cooperators with the Universal Will-To-Good. So we cannot continue to point the finger at the mental darkness of the human race as our excuse for not living in the reality of wholeness.

The crux of the problem, in my opinion, is our sense of priorities. It comes down to what is truly important to us, and for some, living in the dark night of the soul is the perfect place to be. In such self-created experiences, we do not have to take responsibility for our ailments and afflictions. We can say, "Well, you know, I'm going through another one of those dark nights of the soul, and I'll just keep on going until this passes and I see the light again." And we speak such words with our hand on the light switch. (A woman in

California once told me that she did not want a healing of her body because if she was well again, she would have to go to work. She chose the dark night to be free of having to face the responsibilities of service and creative expression.)

Knowing that any kind of darkness in life has been caused by our own resistance in the circuits, it seems to me that we have the responsibility—if we so choose—to make the necessary adjustments in consciousness, using whatever tool is available. If it has to do with a blown fuse in another life, then let's go back to that incarnation and make the correction through understanding. I have seen the reason for, and the opportunity to heal, old wounds from long ago, thus giving me a boost on the spiral toward ultimate freedom and wholeness.

If it takes a greater comprehension of the energies and forces impacting us, then we have the obligation to learn about the causal powers and how they work in consciousness to bind or free us. Jan and I have had major breakthroughs by identifying the living energies within and working to withdraw ego projections from those 22 archetypes that we call *Angels*. We have also devoted countless hours to meditating on the Holy Master Self to draw more of the Spiritual Consciousness into personality, and have used a broad variety of other techniques and formulas to open the flow. And in every situation, we discovered new and powerful expressions of Light, Heat, and Power. I am not trying to set us up as role models; I am simply pointing out that each one of us has some personal work to do in clearing consciousness, and we must not neglect that responsibility.

For example, resistance in the circuits may be traced to attitudes and actions in relationships. Scan your consciousness to feel any relationship blips—husband, wife, son, daughter, father, mother, friends, acquaintances, associates (present and former)—anyone and everyone on this side of the veil and beyond. A strong, hot, emotionally reactive blip tells you that you are generating a force that will ultimately return to you as some kind of an imbalance in your life.

Generally speaking, allergies relate to a misuse of the energy of loving relations—being touchy and oversensitive because of feelings of low self-esteem. Cancer deals with a block in the energy of unconditional love, caused by self-pity, grief, and resentment in personal relations. Diabetes may result from a misuse of the energy of discernment through impulsive behavior and the desire to control relationships. Heart problems may occur because of a block in the energy of strength, thus producing a "struggle-through-life" state of mind that repels productive and rewarding relationships, leading to further futility. Lung problems relate to the energy of loving relations and the grief experienced through the improper choice of a love partner, and the subsequent ending of the relationship. Stomach and intestinal problems can often be traced to a block in the energy of wisdom, frequently caused by irrational acts in relationships and emotional instability; also by an indifference to the emotional needs of others.

Remember that the healing and wholeness of the physical body is important if we are to carry out our part of the Divine Plan. We need to be "in shape" to reveal the *natural* world of peace, love, forgiveness, and understanding. And we have the responsibility to live life to the fullest during this incarnation as an example and inspiration to others—so that they, too, may awaken to Heaven on Earth as a Natural Reality.

~❊~ *4*

THE POWER OF
FAITH IN HEALING

*F*aith is a word that leaves many people a little
cold, primarily because they think of it as an
anemic concept—a rejection of reasoning. To others, it is used as an excuse, a scapegoat, the object
of finger-pointing when prayer does not work. A
woman once told me that the biggest problem with
prayer was that you "have to have too much faith
to make it work, and when I'm hurting, I just can't
believe enough to make the pain go away." Many
of us give up in despair because we feel that our
lack of faith has closed the door to the good that
we so desperately seek.

What we do not understand is that we already
have all the faith we could possibly need, but we

must learn how to use it. Faith is a light of living intelligence and power within the soul...it is a thinking entity within your consciousness now... and if it is not functioning properly, it is because you have not trained it to do your bidding. This you must do, for Faith is the power that can unite all the other powers in a perfect pattern of mastery and dominion. Faith can dissolve the cords that bind the will, and when the spiritual center of Will is free, the Power of Authority is also released.

Pause for a moment and contemplate the idea of Faith. What does it mean to you? Define it. Hold it in your mind and examine every detail of it. *Faith!* It is the Power that can make you whole, that can move mountains. It is the "substance of things hoped for, the evidence of things not seen." (Heb. II, 11:1) We have been told that "...faith subdued kingdoms, wrought righteousness, obtained promises, stopped the mouths of lions, quenched the violence of fire, escaped the edge of the sword. . ." (Heb. II, 11:33-34) Literally, you can do all things through faith because faith is the connecting link between heaven and earth, between cause and effect. The powerful energy of faith will break down the middle wall of partition. The incredibly awesome force of this power will penetrate into the depths of consciousness and burn away the hardened strata of error thought (fear and unbelief).

When you call the Power of Faith into expression, it attracts universal energy and substance to become a powerful inner force. When it reaches spiritual maturity, it begins its work to restore the subconscious mind to its original state of spiritual consciousness—to be in harmony with your super-consciousness.

Faith is indeed the key to mastery because it represents all that you are in Truth. Say to yourself with feeling:

> *I choose to believe that I am more than human. I choose to believe that I am a spiritual being, created in the image and likeness of God. I choose to believe that the Infinite Presence and Power of the Universe has individualized as me, as the Reality of me, as my true nature. I believe that all that the Father is, I am, and all that the Father has is mine. I believe that the I AM of me is God in expression, a consciousness of wholeness, power, and dominion. I believe that I AM the Knowledge of Truth, therefore, I AM the*

Faith of God made manifest. I AM FAITH.

Because I AM Faith, I HAVE Faith, and I feel the spiritual energy of Faith throughout my being now. I will care for my Faith, feeding it with thoughts of the Kingdom, of the Power, and the Glory. In my heart it will grow strong and vibrant and powerful, and will move quickly to unite with its True Self, the Spirit of Truth, my very own Superconsciousness. I will then behold myself as I am in Truth.

The stream of thoughts that continually flow through your mind come from your faith faculty. Remember, these are not *your* thoughts. They are the words and images of this living, thinking entity within you called Faith. Since this entity is one of *your* powers, it belongs to *you*, and it must be under your control, your management, your supervision. When it sends forth thoughts of illness and affliction, you must discipline it immediately, because its word is law, and it can hold you in less-than-perfect physical condition unless you take command. Do not condemn it, though. Understand that it has been operating in accordance with appearances for longer than you can imagine, so you must direct its focus to the Christ Truth within. But once it recognizes the Christ, it will become the organizing center for all of your other powers.

Faith is the "thinking" center in your mind, and the energy is located in the center of the brain. Its energy waves flow through the brain continuously, and if you are not in control, Faith can lead you into a far country like the prodigal son. But after you have begun to assume control of this faculty, you will notice periods of great joy with no obvious explanation. What has happened is that Faith has touched the Order Center within your consciousness, and you feel that all is "right and good." At other times, you'll feel the energy of great enthusiasm, and you will know that Faith is in contact with this faculty. A great warm feeling of love will also signify that Faith is in communication with your Love Center.

Faith is constantly feeding the other power centers with "food" that it is accepting as true. This is why you must teach it to concentrate on Truth thoughts, and when its mind wanders to reflect on ailments and maladies, call it back to view things from the highest vision—the ideal body—nothing but wholeness and perfection. Since Faith is your thinking power, its thoughts must be trained to be loving, wise, enthusiastic, powerful, strong, for-

giving, orderly, understanding, imaginative, filled
with life, and in tune with the will of God. Then,
all the power centers will be united, and your subconscious will be filled with the Light of Spirit.

If your body requires healing now, say:

> *I place my faith in the Christ Mind
> within, knowing that it is even now erasing
> every pattern of disease in my subconscious
> mind and restoring the patterns of perfect
> health. My faith opens the way for the heal-
> ing work of Spirit, and I am healed. I see
> this Truth. I feel it. Therefore, it is done!*

Place your faith in the indwelling Christ. . .and
keep working daily to move up to the level of "no
concern." Make your demonstration, and move past
the trials and tribulations of physical distress. Then,
as your consciousness expands, a treatment for
physical healing will not be required—because you
will be working to demonstrate faith in your God-
Self in order to bring forth all the good that God has
for you now. You will be taking the Christ within,
your True Self, as your All-Sufficiency in every
activity of life—including health and wholeness.

SELECTED EXCERPTS ON HEALTH AND WHOLENESS

The Law of Wholeness

The Law is the action or activity of God—of your Higher Self. You are a center of consciousness through which the Power of God flows. When you turn within and touch the realm of Spirit, your outer mind becomes a channel for the Power. The Power is the Law. It is the action of God Mind. It is Substance. It is Light. It is the Thought Energy—the very Thought Energy of your Higher Self. This Self is always thinking thoughts of perfection. . .perfect health, perfect order, the perfect solution to every problem, the perfect answer to every need. It sees health instead perfect answer to every need. It sees health instead of illness, life instead of death. It sees total fulfillment for you, as you, and this Perfect Pattern of fulfillment is manifest now as your true nature. You are the Self-expression of the Infinite. God has fulfilled Itself as you.

These thought patterns of perfection are focused within you now as the Christ of you, in a Superconsciousness of Sonship, as the Spirit of Truth. But you must recognize and accept this Idea before it can become objectified in your world. Until you embody the Truth, this spiritual energy must flow through a consciousness of imperfection.

Your consciousness is your free will. You are free to think and feel as you choose, but in doing so, you are conditioning the flow according to your own limited thoughts. In essence, the Law becomes your servant. Even though it will flow from the Christ Center on a mission of the highest Vision, it will change its purpose, objective, and destination according to the tone of your consciousness. In the Mind of your Higher Self is the perfect body idea, and this idea of a perfect body is forever expressing itself, sending forth the perfect image into every cell and organ of your body. But again, the Creative Energy must flow through your consciousness, and if your mental atmosphere is charged with a belief in sickness, then the Law will attract sickness to you. Remember what Jesus said—"As a man thinketh in his heart, so is he." You are what you think.

Much effort and discipline are required in controlling the conscious mind, because it is this phase of mind that feeds the subconscious. The subjective realm is totally impersonal. It does not judge. It accepts what you think and believe is true and sets up a vibration that corresponds to that particular concept. That vibration is like a slide in a projector. When the light moves through the slide, the image is projected on the screen. When the energy flows through the field of vibration, the image is projected on the outer screen of life.

You have a conscious phase of mind with which you make decisions. It is the "chooser" in your mental world. Your subconscious is subjective to your conscious mind. It accepts what you think and believe and sets up a vibration for every conviction you have. The combined vibrations make up the total pitch of our soul consciousness.

You have a Superconsciousness, which is your spiritual nature, and the law, emanating from this consciousness of Truth, moves constantly through the vibration field of your mind. There it takes on your now-identity and reproduces this consciousness in your body and affairs. When your thoughts, beliefs, and feelings are in tune with your Truth Center, there is a mind-of-one-vibration. That is the Supermind of each individual, where nothing is impossible.

Living Our Truth of Being

You must remember that you are whole and complete right now. Your Universal Fullness is not something to come; it already is, and that is the absolute Truth that you must *live*. To deny that Truth by playing the misery-loves-company game, or by comprising your spiritual integrity just to please others and be nice and be loved, or by not living *with enthusiasm* the qualities of Self, is to give the Law a fake I.D.—and for this violation you will be arrested.

Your consciousness, which is your life, will be confined to the limits of your false identification through the Law of Attraction, which will bring into your experience all those "human" problems with which you have personally identified. The

Kingdom is finished, and for it to become manifest in Earth as it is in Heaven, it must not only come through you but *as* you. The *as* is the key word because it directly corresponds to your livingness, which is another way of saying that if you do not *live* health, you will not have that experience on a permanent basis.

To live (the verb) means to be alive, to have being, to be! It is being spirited, animated, eager, enthusiastic, buoyant, active, vigorous, and alert. To *be* health, you must totally identify with the Wholeness you already are. You stop paying so much attention to the physical body, and you take the idea of Absolute Well-Being and become it. You "soak" yourself with the Idea from top to bottom, inside and out, day in and day out. You let the dynamic energy of Wholeness saturate your mind and animate your feeling nature, and you continuously live and move and have your being in this invigorating and nourishing Force Field of radiant perfection. You breathe only wellness; you think only perfect health; you feel only hardihood; you speak only words of completeness. You *live* health. You *live* your natural state of being eagerly, enthusiastically, and vigorously. You stay poised and confident, detached from all appearances of sickness and disease in the world, keeping your mind in tune with the spiritual understanding of Absolute Wholeness radiating from your Perfect Self.

You do not commiserate with anyone regarding illness, for you never recognize anything but perfection in another. If a member of your family becomes ill, you do whatever is necessary to lovingly serve as a healing agent—spiritually and on every other level that is necessary. But you continue to be divinely indifferent, lovingly detached, and totally SELF-conscious—standing firm in your Truth and speaking words that reflect only the Truth. You practice harmlessness for you *and* the other person by working totally in the Light of Truth.

Precautions for Better Health

Do not be overly exacting, overly careful, or overly mental. Practice the sacred art of relaxation, of being careless.

Do not engage in lamentation toward self, or accept the herd belief in physical deterioration.

Turn away from selfishness, greediness, ill-nature, malevolence, resentment, and hateful criticism. Be not caught in the whirlpool of alternating suppression and unrestrained desire fulfillment.

Strive for balance. Find the right proportions in life. See symmetry. Be at peace and develop order. When there is harmony, wholeness lives. Without harmony, the door to sickness is open.

Do not accept aging as a principle, or you will age.

Do not satisfy the desires of life through the substitution of food for the fulfillment of other yearnings, or the bones will suffer.

Do not refuse to see Spirit within as the cause of all reality, or there will be friction in mind to affect the bloodstream.

Do not feel irritation toward a class or race or people or feel that you are abused, or you will be vulnerable to infections.

These points, or precautions, simply reflect the ancient teachings on how to stay well on the journey through life.

The Perfect Body Archetype

Has a physical ailment flagged your attention? In the Mind of Self there are no imperfections, and a belief in sickness is nothing more than that—a belief. So you begin by changing your mind and believing the Truth that Healthfulness is the only Reality. You meditate on the Truth that God is the only Health there is, and you link up with the Original Pattern of Perfection—and you stay there until the Fire of Truth burns in your heart and the energy is released into the physical system.

Thoughts and feelings establish vibrations in consciousness, and every thought—particularly ones with an emotional charge—gathers energy, for energy forever follows thought and adapts itself to the nature of the thought.

If you see your body as whole and perfect in your imagination, and *feel* that Wholeness, you are creating a thought-form that will continually be fed with energy. Energy is life, power, and intelligence. Therefore, the thought-form comes alive as a powerful and perceptive entity conscious of itself as a whole and perfect body. It was given birth in your consciousness, and there it will remain—growing, maturing, pulsating, serving you—unless later destroyed by you.

Because it is the nature of every living thing to seek out a vibration similar to its own, the thought-form begins to gravitate toward the Source of Life, the Central Sun of your Force Field, the Master

Self within. In time it finds the Divine Counterpart, the perfect body Archetype established in God Mind. As the ideal meets the Real, a bridge is established enabling the currents of wholeness to flow through the centers (chakras) to affect purification of the glands. If the imaged thought-form is not separated from the Divine Pattern of Perfection through a denial of wholeness, the circulation will continue, and the healthfulness will be maintained.

A Health Lesson from Divine Consciousness

You cannot possess health any more than you can possess illness, for you can only have that which I AM. I am neither health nor illness. I am perfection; therefore, the part of myself that you are is perfect. If you will meditate on your oneness with me and become aware of me as the purity of your being, you will be free of the idea of imperfection. . .my Light will move through your awareness and remove the shadow of the illness. No, the illness is not replaced with health. The Light does not reveal a form of disease and heal it. It simply reveals the *absence* of any imperfection.

The primary process of disease are beliefs

born and nurtured in the emotional nature through a trend of inharmonious living. You may say that whenever energy is blocked, and circulation through the centers is inhibited by a disposition toward conflict, dissension, hostility, pockets of darkness form in the physical system affecting the glands and leading to disease. While there is no incurable disease, it will remain in or near the body until the purification is complete, or as long as the lower nature is out of control, and until the emotional system is transmuted. If you would have wholeness, *be* whole in living. Through meditation on the Christ *within*, the lower faculties begin to glorify the Lord and become receptive to the Light. Where there is Light, there is no darkness, no imperfection.

A Promise from the Holy Self

I have promised you wholeness, saying, as it is written, that I am the Lord your healer, that I heal all your diseases, restore health to you, and heal your wounds. This is not to come. It is. In truth, you are healed now. . .you are whole.

To those who revere my name, the sun of

righteousness shall rise with healing in its wings. Think on this and see the simple instructions. A single eye on the Holy Self within receives Light into consciousness, revealing the absence of disease and the already-present reality of wholeness. I am the Fountain of Healing Life. Will you not drink freely of me?

Proper Diet

The awakened ones have believed for eons that your "diet" is energy—that food is for the etheric body and not the physical, for the etheric absorbs the energy of the food while the function of the physical is to eliminate the food. (The etheric is that sheath of energy that surrounds the physical.) All eatables are essentially energy, yet the benefits or detriment of the energy elements within the form depend on where you are on the life cycle. Personally, I take no thought for what I eat and let the inner Intelligence select the nourishment. I believe that fanaticism in dieting or in the selection of foods is counterproductive to spiritual growth (and wellness).

What you eat or do not eat will not make you

more spiritual. Each individual has different bodily requirements based on his/her ray types, phase of life, and vibratory rates. Eat wholesome food, but pay less attention to your physical body and more to disciplining your *emotional* body. Your physical system will then respond with greater healthiness.

Healing Meditations

Since the attracting vibration (of negative energy) is usually emanating from one of the three lower energy centers, I have found it helpful to start with the root chakra and work up to the crown in a process of transmutation. Focus on the appropriate chakra and meditate on, or audibly affirm, the corresponding ideas.

- *Root chakra at base of spine.*
  In the Mind of God there is only Infinite Perfection, and everything in my life is an expression of that Supreme Wholeness. Nothing comes to me except from the Father. Only that which is pure, good, and fulfilling can enter my world.

- *Spleen chakra below the navel.*
  Divine Order reigns supreme in my life and affairs. All negative emotions are transmuted now, and I am joyous and free as I was created to be.

- *Solar Plexus chakra.*
  The Light of God surrounds me, and I am at perfect peace. I rest in the green pastures and beside the still waters in total serenity.

- *Heart chakra.*
  Only the activity of God is at work in my life, and God is Love. I let God's Love enfold me and care for me now.

- *Throat chakra.*
  The Power of God is my eternal shield. I am totally protected by Omnipotence, now and forever.

- *Third Eye chakra between the brows.*
  The Vision of God is my vision. I see only that which is right, good, and beautiful in my world.

- *Crown chakra.*
  I am illumined in the Christ Consciousness.
  I know only perfection and harmony. I
  feel only peace and love. I see only right
  action and joyful living.

  *The forgiving cleansing love of Christ
  now frees me from all negative thoughts
  and emotions. I turn within and open the
  door to the River of Life and let the healing currents flow through me. I am puri-
  fied and vitalized by this Christ life within.
  I am renewed according to the perfect pattern of Spirit. God sees me as well, whole,
  complete, vibrant, strong, and perfect. And
  so I am!*

Go back and contemplate and ponder upon
each word and sentence. Meditate until you have
an understanding of the ideas behind the words,
and then move on to the next sentence. As your
consciousness becomes in tune with this Truth, it
will shift from a focus on illusion to a centering on
Reality. Your consciousness of God *as* your health
becomes your wellness, your wholeness, your perfection.

*I do not have to treat metaphysically for a healthy body, for the Self that **I AM** is eternally whole and perfect. My consciousness of this Truth is my Health, so I quit paying so much attention to my physical form. I place my focus on the Presence of God **I AM** and the invisible Energy Field that is my Divine Body. Spirit is the Energy of all form, and I let Spirit form Its physical structure as It sees fit. The physical body is no longer any of my business.*

~ 6

A Program for Healing and Wholeness

Let's look at your particular belief system. Do you believe in a Higher Power of Infinite Goodness operating in your life? If you say yes, then your life must be totally fulfilled right now and you are experiencing an all-sufficiency of all good. If you say yes, but your life is not whole and harmonious, you are only thinking and assuming that you believe in the One Presence and Power. You see, in order to determine what you really believe—or the *degree* of your beliefs—you must look at your world, because beliefs are forever externalized. Your world always mirrors your convictions.

To put it rather bluntly, if you are ill, you do

not believe wholeheartedly in God as the Life of your body and your eternal Wellness. Understand that a belief is a point of conscious energy pulsating to a certain vibration within the sphere of its own realm of possibility/probability. This means that there are varying *degrees* of belief, with the externalization reflecting the exact degree.

Think of a rheostat controlling the light of a lamp. As you rotate the knob, there is greater illumination in the room. As you reverse the process, the room becomes darker. The light in the room is directly related to the setting of the rheostat. Now consider the idea that each belief in your overall belief system operates in similar fashion to the rheostat. When the belief is total and complete, it is outpictured in all its fullness at a level (or degree) of 100 percent. But there are also "settings" ranging backwards from 100—that is, 90-80-70-60-50-40-30-20-10, down to zero, or total unbelief.

Apply this illustration to your physical condition. On a scale of 0 to 100, rate your belief setting for health. Say to yourself, *I believe that God is expressing through me now as my perfect health and well-being*—then jot down your present degree of belief, considering both your intuitive feelings and the appearance of a less-than-perfect physical system. Now let's see what we can do to change the "dial set" from degrees of partial belief to the full radiance of absolute conviction.

The "How" of Turning Up the Rheostat

Psychologists say that *thinking* about something is quite different from *believing* it, and that a thought or idea can become a belief positioned in consciousness as a reality only if it remains uncontradicted. (Think how many times each day you deny your good by contradicting what you want to believe.)

William James, founder of one of the first psychological laboratories in this country, said that a belief can be embodied in consciousness through "the path of emotions" and "the path of will." Regarding the emotions, he wrote that the idea or concept must first appear "both interesting and important." The idea, therefore, must be one that excites and stimulates our interest. The interest will then stimulate the emotions—particularly feelings of love, and when the feeling reaches the state of "passion," it is recorded as a belief in the mind.

Concerning "the path of will," he wrote: "Gradually our will can lead us to the same results by a very simple method. We need only *act* as if the thing in question was real, and keep acting as if it were real, and it will infallibly end by growing into such a connection with our life that it will become real. It will become so knit with habit and emotion that our interest in it will be those which characterize belief."[1]

To strengthen the belief in wholeness and health, let's combine the two paths in a seven-step program:

Step #1: The first thing we must do is clear out the negative energy of resentment in our consciousness. (I know we've done this before in earlier chapters, but let's do it again.) I have found that this particular frequency of energy is a most destructive force in not only tearing down positive beliefs, but in also creating the greatest possible variety of fears. Resentment is defined in the dictionary as "a feeling of indignant displeasure at something regarded as a wrong, insult, or injury." How do we eliminate resentment? Go to your dictionary again and look up "forgive"—which is defined as "to cease to feel resentment against—to give up resentment."

The beautiful thing about forgiving is that your deeper-than-conscious mind will act to release you from the attachment of resentment even if you only *want* to forgive and cannot at the time evoke the feeling of loving forgiveness in your heart. In other words, the *will to forgive* is sufficient to begin the cleansing action. Know that any kind of resentment (unforgiveness) toward anyone or anything is blocking your physical wholeness; you can now *want* to forgive through your power of will.

Open your spiritual journal to the next blank page, date it, and start listing everything and anyone you can possibly think of that/who has ever caused you "indignant displeasure." Go back as far as you can remember and write down every hurt, every insult, every mental-emotional-physical injury received from someone. Think of the people, places, situations, and conditions that you have disliked and write them down. Think of every experience that has polluted your consciousness with negative energy, and add it to your list. And if you do not have the following on your list, please add them: your parents, your children, everyone who has been on this planet and who is here now, your world, God, and yourself. Totally forgive all!

When your inventory is complete, start right at

the top and slowly move down the list, bringing each image into your mind and saying:

I forgive you completely. I hold no unforgiveness back. My forgiveness for you is total. I am free and you are free."

Once you have completed this cleansing action, make a note in your journal that beginning now you will continue your forgiveness work by forgiving everyone who you feel has not been released from your emotional attachment. Make a habit to spend a few minutes every single evening at bedtime to forgive those who still cause a dip in your consciousness, plus anyone from that particular day who has caused you "indignant displeasure." Do not go to sleep with any unforgiveness in your heart.

Step #2: Write the following statement in your journal:

I want to believe with all my heart that the One Presence and Power of the Universe is in total control of my mind, my emotions, my body—my entire life. I want to believe in God as the omnipotent healing power and the one source of all my good.

Speak these words aloud, then again silently. Remember that energy follows thought, so as you ponder these words with great feeling, know that the pure energy of this desire is penetrating into your consciousness to do its creative work. It is important that you repeat this statement as often as possible during the first day of the new program— preferably every hour.

Step #3: Totally explore your consciousness, and write in your journal what you think you believe about the healing power of God.

Step #4: Answer this question in your journal: "What is my relationship to God at the present time?" Let your thoughts flow.

Step #5: Answer this question according to your present understanding: "How do I think the Presence of God within would describe Its relationship with me?"

Step #6: Open your heart and mind, and answer this question fully: "What kind of relationship with God do I choose?"

Step #7: Through our focus on our oneness with Spirit—healing the sense of separation with the one relationship so that we may return to wholeness, we are now ready to use a form of the Manifestation Process. It is suggested that you follow this treatment sequence until you demonstrate Spirit as your health.

Go to a quiet place, sit up straight, and take several deep breaths to clear your mind and settle your emotions.

Now imagine that someone has walked up behind you and is standing there looking at you. You feel the stare, and you are so aware of this presence that the entire vibration of your feeling nature is beginning to change. Imagine now that this presence is invisible, a Being of Light and an all-knowing Mind, and that the Presence is slowly moving into you, penetrating your body, your mind, your emotional nature, and your entire consciousness with Itself. Feel the surge of power as this Being of Light and Love moves in to occupy the same space that you do. Sense the intense Knowingness of Its Mind as It thinks within your consciousness. See the Light saturating your entire being.

Understand that through this exercise you have become aware of your God-Self, the Spirit of God within you. Now let's continue with the Manifestation Process.

Say to yourself:

The Spirit of God within is my health and wholeness. I choose now to experience the radiant perfection that is my divine birthright.

Focus on each word with great clarity and then say to yourself:

I accept the experience of radiant health. With all my mind, all my heart, all my soul, I accept this fulfillment now. And because I have accepted my complete wellness, I now have it. I now have the conscious link with spiritual health, which means that my body is responding with new vigor, vitality, and well-being. I AM radiant wholeness!

Now in the chamber of your imagination, see yourself totally enjoying the strength and stamina of wonderful healthfulness. See yourself awakening in the morning and joyfully greeting the new day with a powerful sense of well-being—and continuing throughout the day seeing yourself free of aches and pains and living life to the fullest in perfect health. With controlled visualization, imagine what it means to live in complete wholeness. Create the scenario and believe in it, for what you see you shall become. That's the law!

After several minutes of visualizing your vibrant health and happiness, say to yourself with great feeling:

> *O how I love what I see. I love the joyous expressions and the happy scenes. I love my hale and hearty body, my active, invigorating life—doing what I love and loving what I do. I love the pictures of total fulfillment that I am now seeing in my mind and feeling in my heart.*

Now close the curtain on the screen of your mind and turn within to the Spirit of God, the Reality of you, and let the feeling of that Presence enter your heart. Say to yourself, aloud if possible:

Nothing is too good for me to have or experience, so in the name and through the power of my Holy Self, I speak the word. I let there be perfect physical health now! I let the healing power of God come forth into manifestation here and now. I let the Spirit of God work in and through me to express as wholeness in my body, peace in my emotions, and joy in my mind. In the name of Christ, I am whole and perfect, and it is so!

And silently:

I now totally and completely surrender to the activity of God, the only power at work in my life. I let go and let God be God. I let go and let the Spirit of God do Its perfect work in and through me.

Thank you, my Beloved Sacredness, for this new life of wholeness. Thank you for my radiant health. My heart overflows with gratitude and joy. Praise God! Praise God! Praise God!

Now you are ready to move into action, which is necessary to maintain the belief system at the highest level until it "locks in" as a complete realization. And this is where "the path of will" comes into play. Recall the role that you assumed in your creative visualization where you devoted the day to enjoying your radiant health and wholeness. This is what you must do now in actual practice. And you must play the role with all the emotion, excitement, fullness of heart, and love that you can feel. Remember that "when the feeling reaches the stage of *passion,* it is recorded as a belief in the mind." And as you're doing this, talk with Spirit, laugh with Spirit, play with Spirit, love with Spirit—and in your oneness with Omniscience and Omnipotence, your ideal body will become Real for you—and you will remember only in the faint recesses of your mind that other person you were who had accepted a less-than-perfect physical condition.

Now you complete the process by seeing every individual only as the perfect Being of God, recognizing nothing but radiant wholeness in every person regardless of appearances. Through this highest vision, you will be seeing *yourself,* and your body will continue to maintain its natural condition of beautiful wellness.

❧ 7

HEALING OTHERS

L ate one evening on the hillside where we lived, I was so filled with love for Earth, her people, and all forms of life, that I suddenly exclaimed in a loud voice, "God bless this world!" And then I thought about what I had said, wondering about the audacity of directing the Source from Whom all blessings flow to do something that was *already* being done. If one believes in an eternally loving and constantly giving Omnipresence, and I do, then what does it mean to "bless" a person or a planet?

As I was contemplating these thoughts, I experienced a "flow-through" that said, "The act of blessing another is to offer yourself as a channel for the activity of Spirit. When you bless an individual, a form, or a situation, you become the instrument through which divine energy flows to adjust, heal, and elevate consciousness."

Think about that. To bless is to connect the radiation of Self (the *I*) and the object of the blessing in a focused cord of light. Jesus came into this world to bless it, offering himself as a Divine Channel for Supreme Being. This is our role, too—even before we reach his level of consciousness. We begin where we are to do our part in reconnecting the third and fourth dimensions—to be a conduit between Earth and Heaven for the dynamic Will of God.

To bless someone or something is so much more than muttering words of endearment or finding another way of expressing gratitude. In truth, it is taking an action in consciousness with words to lift the recipient of the blessing back up to the Divine Standard of Harmony. So the next time you utter a blessing, think about what you are doing. Focus the mind to channel the energy, open your heart to make the connection with the object of the blessing, and speak the words to release the power.

There is no manipulation involved, no attempt to influence or interfere with free will, so you need not wait until you are asked for assistance to give your blessings. Just bless everyone and everything, including yourself. And when you hear someone blessing you, just remember that you are being touched by the Light and Love of *I*—the Omnipotent Spirit of God—through the person conferring the blessing.

The Healing Currents

An extension to the act of blessing is the actual physical healing of others. When you have evolved in consciousness to the point where the *I* is realized, one requiring assistance simply says to you, "I need your prayers." A connection in consciousness will have been made, and the one seeking help receives the healing without effort on your part. Remember, it is the Master within Who heals. Until we have the Realization Experience, however, we work from where we are—regardless of how faint our awareness of the God Presence may be. Just know that even if a flicker of the healing light gets through a crack in our opaqueness, a positive benefit will occur. And the more transparent we are, the greater the results. Sometimes the effects are immediate; at other times the harmonizing of the situation is gradual—but in retrospect, it is seen as the logical working out of a problem according to cosmic law.

Here is one example of a highly effective method that may be used if someone asks for your prayers. Go into a meditative state to realize as clearly as possible the reality and perfection of your own Inner Self. Contemplate with "relaxed intensity" the attributes of the Infinite *I,* the God-Self that you are. Ponder the incredible Love, the infinite Wisdom, the perfect Life, the radiant Light, the dynamic Will, the awesome Power, the absolute Truth.

As the feeling of the Presence begins to expand in your consciousness, pour all the love of your being into that Presence. Let love fill you and wash over you and spill out before you until love is the dominant vibration of your entire consciousness. At that point, gently bring the individual who has asked for your prayers into your awareness. See the individual clearly, or if you do not know the individual personally, simply see his or her name in a circle of light. Now begin to flood that person (or the name in the circle) with your love. See the love flowing from you in streams of radiant energy, literally saturating and enveloping the person or circle. Keep radiating the love and watching the scene in your mind until the object is seen only as a brilliant energy field of Love-Light. Now slowly withdraw your attention, as if moving away from the object, and consciously release the person to Spirit. The more you practice this technique, the more proficient you will become.

Another method that has produced seeming miracles is almost like the above process in reverse. You begin with the person's name or face etched firmly in your mind, and lovingly contemplate the individual. After a moment or two, begin to meditate on *your* Truth of Being, your Holy Self, and keep at it until the person or name completely disappears from consciousness and your entire focus is on the Presence within. Even if you can only "forget" the individual for a few seconds while your mind is totally on God, the results will be amazing. The reason: The individual moved out of your human consciousness into the pure Essence of Spirit where no disease or lack exists.

One particular healing group I know of uses a process they call "window cleaning." They work on the inner planes to effect a cleansing of the person's energy field and alter the vibrational pitch, thus removing the blocks that may have unconsciously been imposed. When the individual is clear of these pockets of misqualified energy, the Spiritual Self shines through in all its glory to straighten out the crooked places and make all things new. Understand that praying for others or altering vibrations is not performing magic, and neither is it giving someone a "fix"—you are a metaphysician, not a meta*fixer*. This absent healing work is simply cooperating with Spirit for the benefit of another.

Our ongoing research at The Quartus Foundation tells us that the results of prayers and spiritual treatments on behalf of others may only be temporary, that unless the consciousness that produced the problem in the first place is changed, the negative situation may reoccur. This is why I so strongly emphasize to others the vital importance of daily spiritual study, prayer and meditation, listening to the inner Voice, journal writing, thought management, emotional control, harmlessness in actions, communing with Nature, and living the highest Truth. We all came back into physical form to awaken to our true Identity and move above the woes and sorrows of the third dimension, and we must not let anything stand in the way of fulfilling that mission and purpose. At the same time, we must never forget another reason that we are here on Planet Earth: *We are here to be of service to humanity and to do all that we can to assist our brothers and sisters to awaken from the dream state.* And if that requires a healing in mind and body, let's do it with love and joy, and with gratitude for the opportunity to serve.

8

HEALING THOUGHTS TO PONDER

*There is a Power within me that is
responsive to my needs. When I make
conscious contact with this Power, it will
literally transform my life because in my
true nature, I am this Power in expression.
I am now consciously aware of the Power.*

*God is my perfect health, and as I realize
this Truth, it will be reflected in my body.
My consciousness of God as my health
IS my health!*

I am alive because I am Life. My Life is God's Life. My Life is God. I feel my livingness within me. I feel God.

I am complete. I am whole. Because God is expressing as me, there is nothing missing in my life. I release all fear and doubt and lift up my vision to behold my Self as I am in Truth.

Every single experience in my life— whether "good" or "bad"—is created out of the vibration of my consciousness. The higher the vibration, the greater the degree of Good in my life. I understand this now.

If I continually think about the possibility of being attacked by some form of disease, then I am developing a

*consciousness of disease, which must out-
picture itself as a breakdown of the body.
I no longer think such thoughts.*

*I do not work to develop a healthier body.
Rather, I work to gain a consciousness of
health, a spiritual consciousness
of wholeness.*

*The dynamic movement of Creative
Energy is taking place now, in and
through me. My Spirit knows exactly what
to do, and is doing it now. That which
concerns me has been perfected, and I
am now whole, strong, and free.*

*God does not cause, will, or authorize
sickness. All disease and physical illness
can be traced to inhibiting the Life Force
radiating from the Master Self within.*

I no longer inhibit the Light of Life.
I shine as the Holy Sun and enjoy
my radiant wholeness.

I am not a physical body. I am the
sum-total of all energies in expression as
Pure Consciousness. I live above
the physical vehicle.

I am love, I am loved, I am loving. I feel
the love vibration in my heart. I feel it
expanding throughout my body.
All there is, is love. . .love. . .love.

My world is simply my consciousness
projected on the screen of life, and
anything I see that is not in perfect har-
mony is not the Will of God;
therefore, it is not real.

I meditate on Spirit as the restoring power in every cell and organ, the pure holy Life of my body, as energy, vitality, and wholeness.

Closer than breathing is the Presence of God I AM—absolute harmony, perfect love, infinite wisdom—the only power, the only cause, the only activity of my eternal life.

It is fun to be healthy. I live in the joy of wholeness.

Notes

**CHAPTER TWO: The Divine Vibration
of Wholeness**
   1. Louise L. Hay, *Heal Your Body* (Carlsbad, CA.:
Hay House, Inc., 1988), p. 3.

CHAPTER SIX: A Program for Healing and Wholeness
   1. John Randolph Price, *Practical Spirituality* (Carlsbad,
CA.: Hay House, Inc., 1996), pp. 66–67—in reference to
GREAT BOOKS OF THE WESTERN WORLD, Vol. 53,
William James (Chicago: Encyclopedia Britannica Inc.,
1952).

ABOUT THE AUTHOR

John Randolph Price is an internationally known author and lecturer, and has devoted over 25 years to researching the philosophic mysteries of ancient wisdom and incorporating those revelations in the writing of more than a dozen books. His work has earned national and international awards for humanitarianism, progress toward global peace, and contributing to a higher degree of positive living throughout the world.

In 1981, he and his wife, Jan, formed The Quartus Foundation, a spiritual research and communications organization. And on December 31, 1986, they launched the first World Healing Day, which continues each year.

For information about workshops, the annual Mystery School conducted by John and Jan Price, and their monthly publications, please contact:

The Quartus Foundation
P.O. Box 1768, Boerne, Texas 78006
Telephone: 830-249-3985 • Fax: 830-249-3318
E-mail: quartus@texas.net
Quartus Web page:
http://lonestar.texas.net/~quartus

We hope you enjoyed this Hay House book. If you would like to receive a free catalog featuring additionalHay House books and products, or if you would like information about the Hay Foundation, please contact:

Hay House, Inc.
P.O. Box 5100
Carlsbad, CA 92018-5100

(760) 431-7695 or **(800) 654-5126**
(760) 431-6948 (fax) or **(800) 650-5115 (fax)**

Please visit the Hay House Website at:
www.hayhouse.com